Ripley's Believe It or Not!

Special Edition 2016

■ SCHOLASTIC

Trade ISBN 978-0-545-85279-1
School Market ISBN 978-0-545-89073-1

10 9 8 7 6 5 4 3 2   15 16 17 18 19/0

Printed in China   62
First printing 2015

PUBLISHING

Developed and produced by Ripley Publishing Ltd.

Publisher: Anne Marshall
Editorial Director: Becky Miles
Art Director: Sam South
Senior Designer: Michelle Foster

Project Editor: Charlotte Howell
Senior Researcher: James Proud
Design: Rocket Design (East Anglia) Ltd.
Indexer: Hilary Bird
Reprographics: Juice Creative

Cover photos ©: Squid, Richard E. Young/Tree of Life web project/tolweb.org; bubbles, tunart/iStockphoto; background, Photocreo Bednarek/Fotolia.

Page 54

Page 105

Contents

Page 80

Page 23

Page 92

The Ripley Effect

In the 1930s and 1940s the Ripley cartoon series was estimated to have reached more than 80 million people, and Ripley received more mail than Santa Claus and the US Presidents.

Robert Ripley, the inspiration behind the *Ripley's Believe It or Not!* books and Odditoriums (museums), spent his life traveling the world in search of the extraordinary. It all began when he started work as a cartoonist in *The New York Globe* in 1918. There Ripley began using real-life stories of the people and places he had seen on his travels as subjects in his cartoons.

Ripley visited more than 200 countries in his lifetime, including Papua New Guinea, Armenia, and China. He used every kind of transport imaginable, including plane, boat, horse, camel, and donkey.

Ripley visited the Taj Mahal in India in 1936, on one of his many rambles around the world.

Ripley's legacy lives on today with 32 Ripley's Odditoriums worldwide, three aquariums, a warehouse packed with incredible artifacts, and an archive of more than 30,000 photos and 125,000 cartoons.

The Ripley cartoons are still drawn daily—making *Ripley's Believe It or Not!* the longest running syndicated cartoon in the world.

The Ripley's team continues today to hunt for the best "believe it or nots!" from around the world. We gather facts from many different sources, including Facebook, Twitter, YouTube, TV, and radio shows—and we also send out researchers to find stories. But some of the most incredible stories are sent to us personally from our Ripley fans.

In 1930, Robert Ripley started broadcasting "Believe It or Not" radio on CBS and NBC, and by 1948, the show had made it onto television.

"I have traveled in 201 countries and the strangest thing I've seen was man."
ROBERT RIPLEY

The first Ripley's Odditorium opened in Chicago in 1933.

The Ripley's Believe It or Not! Odditorium in Branson, Missouri.

A Quest for the New...

Ripley's archivist Edward Meyer, based in our head office in Orlando, Florida, spends most of his year looking for new and incredible exhibits for the many Ripley's Believe It or Not! Odditoriums. And this year is no exception. Here are some of our favorite new artifacts from the Ripley warehouse...

Believe it or not, this dragon is made of plastic cutlery! Made by Wilmer Lam from Orlando, Florida.

A portrait of musician Jimi Hendrix made by Ed Chapman from the UK entirely of guitar picks (plectrums).

James Hawkins from Chicago, Illinois, made this artwork out of different-colored duct tape!

Check out some of these amazing stories inside your book, sent in by our very own Ripley fans!

No wonder she's known as the talon queen!

Page 98

Page 57

Not for the faint-hearted, that's an ice wheelie!

Page 36

Wow, a new tail!

Really?

Keep an eye out for extra Ripley stories bursting through the pages!

Questions, questions...

Watch out for interviews inside!

Ripley's Believe It or Not!

Download our app for free!

If you have a story you think Ripley's would like, get in touch!

Our website: www.ripleys.com/books

Our e-mail: bionresearch@ripleys.com

Our social media: Facebook, Pinterest, Instagram, and Twitter

Or write to us at: BION Research, Ripley Entertainment Inc.,

7576 Kingspointe Parkway, Suite 188, Orlando, Florida, 32819, USA

Chapter 1

Wonderful World

Crazy Climates

Foam's Up

Overflowing floodwaters whipped up the sea at Karitane, New Zealand, to create a layer of foam that stretched for 330 feet across the water. It was almost 100 feet wide in places. The froth did not discourage daring surfers, who dodged debris as they rode the ten-foot waves.

Huge Hailstones

Dang!

Freak hailstones the size of eggs damaged buildings, vehicles, and trees when a storm battered Songxian County in China's Henan Province. Hailstones start as tiny pieces of ice. As air currents carry them up and down through a storm, they collide with water droplets and grow steadily larger.

Glowing Floes

Lake Baikal in Siberia, Russia, is one of the largest, deepest lakes on Earth and holds about one-fifth of the world's freshwater. In winter, changes in temperature and strong winds cause the frozen surface of the lake to crack, forming these strange lumps of turquoise ice.

Really?

Earthquakes can shorten the length of a day by affecting the Earth's rotation. In 2011, a quake in Japan knocked 1.8 microseconds off the length of every day afterward.

Electrifying Image

Photographer Rolf Maeder was planning to take shots of the sunset over the Grand Canyon, but the light was too hazy. On his way home he noticed a storm building, so he set up his tripod. By using a long exposure, he was able to capture this amazing picture of lightning striking the canyon.

Sensational Sights

Sea of Stars

The sparkling blue specks of light on the shoreline of this beach in the Maldives were created by tiny creatures called bioluminescent phytoplankton. They give out light when they are stressed—by lapping waves, for example—and look like a web of glittering stars.

Magical Cave

This bizarre ice cave was carved by a hot water spring flowing beneath a glacier on the volcanic Kamchatka Peninsula, in the far east of Russia. The roof of the cave is so thin that sunlight shines through it, giving the strange ice formations an eerie emerald-green glow.

Nature's Christmas Lights

Canadian photographer Steve Irvine captured this image of thousands of fireflies outside his Ontario home. As the landscape came alive with flickering lights, he set up his camera and began a time-lapse sequence lasting more than an hour. The background streaks were made by stars as the Earth turned.

Fireflies "talk" to one another using light signals.

Sight-seeing Hotspot

Lava-loving tourists have been flocking to an erupting volcano called Plosky Tolbachik in eastern Russia, which burst into action after lying dormant for 36 years. At the height of the eruption, 1,300 tons of lava flowed from the crater every second and clouds of ash reached 33,000 feet into the air.

Festival Spectacle!

Pie in the Sky

The very messy World Custard Pie Championship takes place every year in the village of Coxheath, England. Teams of four, standing eight feet away from one another, throw creamy custard pies at their opponents! Points are awarded for hits to the face, chest, and arms. "The Grannies" took the 2014 crown, beating 2013's winners "Pie and Smash."

More than 2,000 pies were thrown in the 2014 contest!

Mud Madness

At the Boryeong Mud Festival, held on Daecheon Beach, South Korea, you can try mud boxing, mud body painting, and even mud-filled trampolines! The festival attracts thousands of visitors each year who believe the mud, from the city's pure plains, has health benefits, and anyone who's too muddy can always wash off in the ocean.

Walking Dead

In May 2014, a large group of people dressed as scary zombies walked (very slowly) through the streets of London, England. The Zombie Walk, an event that first started in the U.S., now takes place every year in cities all over the world.

Really?

At the Moose Dropping Festival in Talkeetna, Alaska, hundreds of moose droppings are released from the sky onto the town, and locals bet on where they will land.

Grrrr...

Eccentric Chinese professor Zhang Lin shifted tons of rubble and rock onto the roof of a Beijing apartment block to build his dream mountaintop villa.

The world's only toilet-shaped house (made of glass and concrete) is in South Korea and was built by Sim Jae-Duck, who was born in a toilet.

For people with nothing to hide, there is a completely see-through house in Tokyo, Japan.

Home, Sweet Home

This 60-foot-long gingerbread house must be the sweetest property in Texas. Large enough for a family of five, the house has almost 4,000 gingerbread bricks, made from 7,200 eggs, thousands of pounds of flour and sugar, and almost a ton of butter. It was built to raise money for a nearby hospital.

Jet-Set Lifestyle

This Boeing 727 airliner is an unexpected sight among the trees on a suburban plot near Portland, Oregon. It is home to engineer Bruce Campbell, who bought the former passenger jet for about $100,000 back in 1999, and has since converted it into a fully functioning home.

In Brazil, a vertical house has been built on a climbing wall! It includes shelves, a bed, and a hammock.

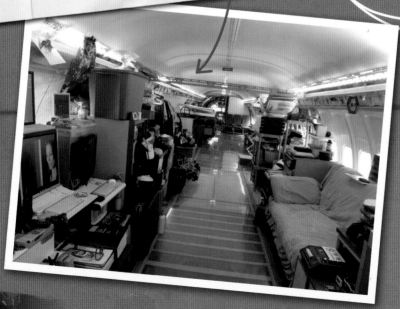

Sleep Tight

Cool Hotel

Visitors get a frosty welcome at the Iglu-Dorf hotel, located at an altitude of 5,900 feet in Switzerland. It takes 3,000 tons of snow to create the igloo hotel, which is rebuilt every year, and rooms feature unique wall art and sculptures carved by international artists.

Power Napping

Tired passersby were able to check in for a free 20-minute nap at this pop-up hotel in Montreal, Canada. The hotel, which has eight sleep pods with mattresses and pillows, was advertising nasal strips to aid breathing at night, but also promoted the benefits of a daytime nap.

Sleep with the Fishes

This hotel room 13 feet below the water is perfect for visitors hoping for a deep sleep. The room is part of an island resort off the east coast of Africa. As well as the underwater bedroom with a panoramic view of a nearby coral reef, there is a water deck for swimming, and a roof deck for stargazing.

Really?

Hotel Movil is a mobile hotel that can be delivered on the back of a truck. Once on site, it expands like a Transformer into a two-story building with 11 rooms and a terrace.

Beachfront Hotel

The Sandcastle Hotel in Weymouth, southern England, is right on the beach, just a stone's throw from the sea. It sounds ideal, but there is no bathroom, and if it rains, the roofless hotel will quickly disappear. Sculptor Mark Anderson built the impressive structure using 1,000 tons of sand.

About 12 percent of the Earth's surface is permanently covered in ice and snow, but this can rise to 33 percent during the Northern Hemisphere's winter.

There are at least 13 different forms of sea ice, including cake ice, brash ice, frazil ice, and pancake ice.

20

the bigger picture!

Winter Wonderland

Temperatures in Harbin, northeast China, dip to minus 31°F in winter, so it is the ideal location for the International Ice and Snow Sculpture Festival. More than 7,000 people work around the clock to carve blocks of ice from the Songhua River into huge sculptures, and even full-size buildings. In 2014, the Festival celebrated its thirtieth anniversary and featured a 150-foot-tall replica of the Hallgrimskirkja church in Reykjavik, Iceland.

Really?

Blood Falls waterfall in Antarctica looks like blood running from a cut in a glacier. The water is rich in iron, which rusts when it meets the air, leaving it the color of blood.

21

Crazy Journeys

Extreme School Run

The mountaintop village of Zhang Jiawan in southern China is cut off from the outside world apart from a series of ladders that lead down the sheer cliffs to the valley below. Children have to climb up and down ladders to get to school and back every day. Without the ladders, the walk to school would take more than four hours.

Tunnel Tree

Sequoia National Park, in the Sierra Nevada mountains of California, is famous for its giant sequoia trees. When one of these majestic trees died and fell across a park road in 1937, workers cut an eight-foot-tall, 17-foot-wide tunnel through the trunk so that the road was passable again.

TUNNEL LOG
LL DECEMBER 4, 1937
SE DIAMETER 21 FEET
LENGTH 275 FEET
L 8 FT. HIGH 17 FT WIDE

Toys in Space

When three children asked their father to send their favorite toys into space, Nicolas Lamorelle ordered a weather balloon and installed cameras on his homemade flying machine to record the journey. The toys, Bad Piggy from Angry Birds and Hello Kitty, reached 65,000 feet above sea level before floating safely back to Earth.

Questions, questions...

We asked Nicolas about the journey...

How did you know if the adventure would work?
My children, Kylian, Kallie, and Inaya, asked me if it was possible to send their toys into space and I had to say no. But then I studied how we would do it and found it was possible. I still did not know it would definitely work—it was a risk—but I knew it would make my children happy.

How did you prepare the toys for their journey?
We had to prepare the toys the day before the release, then we waited to send them up until the last moment. We explained to the children that there was a risk of losing them, but they trusted me and they knew that we would find them.

Were you worried the toys wouldn't make it back?
The toys were much more important than the equipment, so it was very stressful because we had difficulty finding them. The iPhone and GPS had switched off, but luckily the GPS tracker restarted and we found them in a cornfield! We took a blanket for them and finished the day with a family picnic.

Don't look down!

Branching Out

Roar!

The hedge is 20 feet tall!

Terrifying Topiary

A gardener in Norfolk, England, has spent ten years sculpting his hedge into a 100-foot-long dragon with six legs, huge wings, and some sharp teeth. The mythical monster often startles passersby as they walk along the nearby footpath.

Well-Rooted

Trees that grow in shallow rain forest soils often develop huge roots above ground to provide extra food for the tree and keep it in place. They can stretch more than six feet up the trunk and are especially common in Costa Rica, where this photo was taken.

Tree-Trainer

Axel Erlandson was a Swedish-American farmer who shaped trees as a hobby. His famous "circus trees" were real trees grown into unusual shapes using a special technique that Axel never revealed. Some of the giant, twisted trees still remain in Gilroy Gardens in California.

Really?

Plants and trees can warn one another about bug attacks! When bugs chew leaves, some plants release chemical signals to other plants, which then use defensive chemicals against the bugs.

Friendly Giant

Seattle-based artist Kim Beaton and a team of 25 volunteers spent 15 days creating this 12-foot-tall tree troll using papier-mâché, wood, metal plates, and other materials. Trolls are usually quite frightening, but this creature's kind face was inspired by a dream Kim had about her late father.

Harold Hackett puts messages in bottles and throws them into the sea from North Cape, Canada. He has sent more than 5,000 bottles and has had replies from places as far away as Ireland and Honduras.

Long Drop

Around 9,000 caves lie beneath the ground in Tennessee, and the Mystery Falls pit in Chattanooga is one of the most spectacular. Pit caves are vertical shafts, usually created by water and, at 281 feet, Mystery Falls is the deepest waterfall pit cave in the state.

More than 61 tons of silver, worth $36 million, have been recovered from the SS Gairsoppa 70 years after the ship was torpedoed off the coast of Ireland during World War II. There may be up to 240 tons of silver still on board.

Secret City

In 1959, a valley in China's Zhejiang Province was flooded as part of a hydroelectric power project, creating Qiandao Lake. This magical picture shows the lake's secret—the ancient city of Shi Cheng. It was submerged by the water and has been preserved intact, so it is a virtual time capsule.

The flooded valley as it is today.

Akrotiri, a Minoan Bronze Age settlement in Santorini, Greece, was destroyed in a volcanic eruption around 1627 BCE. Ash preserved pieces of artwork, which were rediscovered in 1967.

Naturally Amazing

Incredible Island

Viewed from the air, it is easy to see why the Italian island of Gallo Lungo is nicknamed "Dolphin Island." It is one of three islands off the Amalfi coast where, according to Greek legend, the Sirens tempted Odysseus as he traveled home from war.

Dolphin island is privately owned, and has been home to the rich and famous.

Bear Boulder

The Italian island of Sardinia has become well-known for its rock formations, which have been sculpted by the wind into many strange shapes. They include an elephant, a vulture, human heads, and this rocky polar bear, which sits above the La Maddalena archipelago.

Fire and Ice

Kseniia Maiukova spotted this dragon-shaped iceberg during a tourist boat trip around a bay near Petermann Island, Antarctica. At first, the group thought it looked like a thumb. It was only when they returned to land that they decided it looked just like a dragon.

Frosty Photos

Russian photographer Sergey Makurin captured these otherworldly images of snow-covered trees in the Ural Mountains, where temperatures can drop to minus 35°F. The Urals form the border between Europe and Asia, and they are the oldest mountains in the world.

Chapter 2

Curious Critters

How Big?

Half-Ton Tuna

Fisherman Marc Towers landed the catch of his life off Nova Scotia, Canada. This 1,000-pound bluefin tuna was too heavy to lift onto his boat, so he had to tow it back to shore. The fish is so big that it could be made into 20,000 pieces of sushi!

Super-Sized Rodent

Farmers usually try to get rid of rats, but in China's Guizhou Province they are fattening bamboo rats to sell for meat. The giant rats can grow to the size of a small dog and weigh almost nine pounds. Their meat costs four times more than chicken or pork.

Monster Stinger

Californian photographer Bob Cranston had a close encounter with a rare jellyfish that was twice as big as him while diving in the Pacific Ocean, near Mexico. He admitted that he and fellow diver Howard Hall, pictured here, got too close and were stung by the giant jelly.

Really?

The blue whale is the biggest creature ever to have lived and it's still around today! It weighs up to 200 tons and grows up to 100 feet long—as long as three school buses.

Long Lick

This purebred pug's tongue is almost as long as her legs. The dog, named Penny, was a contestant in the World's Ugliest Dog competition in Petaluma, California. Pugs sometimes suffer from "hanging tongue," which is a minor condition where their tongue hangs out.

Wheeze!

What Are You Doing Here?

Slithery Surprise!

Marlene Swart and Leon Swanepoel, from England, were shocked to find a 16-foot-long, deadly snake hiding out under the hood of their car! The couple were on vacation at the Kruger National Park in South Africa when the huge python slid into the cozy spot.

Big Catch!

This belted kingfisher caught more than a mouthful when it grabbed this large goldfish! It may look like more than he could handle, but the hungry bird managed to swallow the whole thing after just a few attempts. Although, he did need to rest on the branch for a while after his giant lunch!

Tree House

Zhang Fugen's 35 chickens have lived in a tree for five years! They abandoned the hen house Zhang built them in Lanxi, in China's Zhejiang Province, and moved up to the tree. Most of them come down during the day, but some lazy ones stay in the tree all day and night!

Peculiar Playmates

Bubbles, a 9,000-pound rescued orphan elephant, and Bella, a Labrador retriever, live together at Myrtle Beach Safari, South Carolina. They go for walks together and Bella even climbs onto Bubbles' back when they are swimming!

Super Survivors

Winter's Tale

When Winter, a bottlenose dolphin, lost her tail after being caught in a crab trap off the coast of Florida, a team of experts that usually treats human amputees spent 18 months creating an artificial tail to help her swim normally. Winter now lives at Clearwater Marine Aquarium and her story is told in the movies *Dolphin Tale* and *Dolphin Tale 2*.

Questions, questions...

We talked to David Yates, the CEO of Clearwater Marine Aquarium and Executive Producer of the movies, about Winter's incredible story...

What was so difficult about creating Winter's artificial tail?

It was the first time it had ever been done! We literally had to start from scratch and find ways to make it work. The biggest challenge was to keep the tail on Winter's sensitive skin. We finally developed "Winter's gel," a gel that protected her skin and kept the tail in place.

How long did it take to create her tail?

The first tail took about 6 to 7 months to make, but we are still making changes to the tail today and improving it all the time.

Does Winter wear the tail all the time?

Winter is almost nine, and like a human child with a prosthetic leg she wears her tail at times throughout the day, but not all the time. The tail is also great physical therapy for her back.

Kind-Hearted Kayaker

Pentti Taskinen was kayaking on Lake Tuusula, Finland, when he spotted an exhausted northern hawk owl in the icy waters. Pentti lifted the freezing bird onto the front of his kayak and took it ashore. It dried out next to a stove and was later released.

Thanks!

Really?

A bull elephant smashed a house in an Indian village, leaving a baby girl trapped. When she started to cry, the elephant returned and gently removed all the debris from around her with his trunk.

Goat on Wheels

A baby goat named Frostie was brought to Edgar's Mission animal sanctuary near Melbourne, Australia, after losing the use of his hind legs because of an infection. Staff there fitted the week-old kid with a set of rear wheels so he could run around with his new friends.

Squeak...

Human Zoo

Bored office workers have been bringing wildlife into the workplace by lining up their heads with an onscreen photo of an animal's body and posting the silly snaps online. Called "desk safari," the craze started in London, England, and quickly spread worldwide.

A trend called "cat breading" involves cutting a hole in a slice of bread and placing it around a cat's head so it looks like a lion's mane.

Feline 'Fro

Following the Internet craze for cat beards, where people held fluffy cats around their chins, comes the cat Afro—or catfro. The new trend in kitty fashion involves wearing a cat on your head like a wig. Just watch out for the claws!

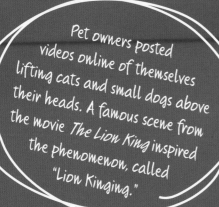

BFFs

Best Buddies

Eight-year-old Matteo Walch has a special relationship with a colony of marmots—creatures that are normally shy around humans. Matteo, from Innsbruck, Austria, has been visiting the marmots in the Austrian Alps for four years. He rubs noses and shares food with his furry friends, who run straight to him as soon as he arrives.

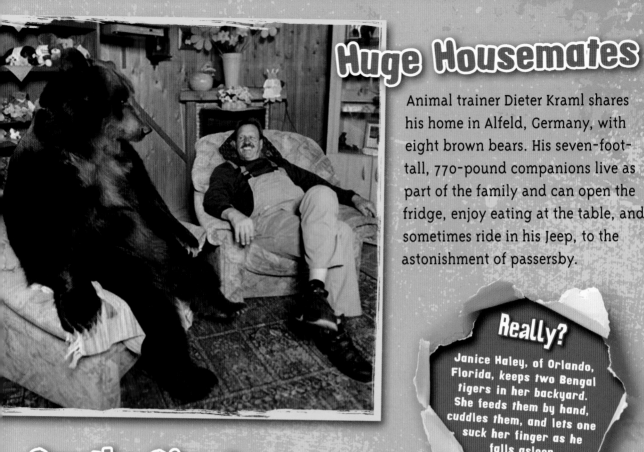

Huge Housemates

Animal trainer Dieter Kraml shares his home in Alfeld, Germany, with eight brown bears. His seven-foot-tall, 770-pound companions live as part of the family and can open the fridge, enjoy eating at the table, and sometimes ride in his Jeep, to the astonishment of passersby.

Really?

Janice Haley, of Orlando, Florida, keeps two Bengal tigers in her backyard. She feeds them by hand, cuddles them, and lets one suck her finger as he falls asleep.

Gentle Giant

Elizaveta Tishchenko has been friends with an orphaned white rhino named Max ever since he was found at the Ol Pejeta Conservancy in Kenya. The two-ton pet could easily charge and crush the 12-year-old, but Max is so gentle he even rolls over so Elizaveta can rub his stomach.

Strange but True

Fluorescent Fish

These angelfish, seen here at a fish farm in Taiwan, have been specially engineered to glow in the dark. At up to six inches long, they are the largest glowing fish in the world that are able to mate and reproduce.

Glow for it!

Open Wide

This fearsome deep-sea creature has what appear to be human teeth! The unusual species of squid, the *Promachoteuthis sulcus*, was discovered at 6,500 feet in the South Atlantic Ocean. But it isn't as scary as it looks, its "teeth" are actually fleshy lips around its beak, and it is only 1-inch long!

Panda Lookalike

John Bartheld, a farmer from Roy, Washington, finally succeeded in his quest to breed a miniature cow with markings like a panda when Peanut was born in 2013. There are fewer than 40 "panda cows" in the world, which makes them even rarer than actual giant pandas.

A miniature cow has to be less than 42 inches tall at three years old to be called a miniature cow.

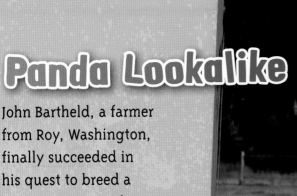

Scary Spider

This mini-beast with its menacing clown-face markings might even scare people who are not afraid of spiders. Ukrainian photographer Igor Ryabov came across the crab spider close to his home, but there's no need to have nightmares—these harmless creatures are less than half an inch long.

43

Superb Skills

Cool Cat

Didga the skateboarding cat lives life in the fast lane as he cruises through the Australian town of Coolangatta on his remote-controlled board. The talented tabby pulls off an array of tricks, too, including jumping on and off the board onto low walls and even leaping over a dog.

Canine Copilot

Callie, a chocolate Labrador, has earned her own crew card after clocking up more than 250 flying hours alongside her owner, British private pilot Graham Mountford. She has now visited most parts of the UK, and is rewarded with a treat when she lands.

Takeoff!

Hogging the Waves

A piglet named Zorro has been riding the waves with his owner Matthew Bell since he was just three weeks old. The pair check out the surf in New Zealand's Bay of Plenty first thing each morning and Matthew plans to keep on doing so until Zorro gets too big for the board.

Heavy Metal

Fourteen jumbo musicians weighing three times as much as a full orchestra are helping to raise funds for an elephant conservation center in Thailand. Dave Soldier, cofounder of the Thai Elephant Orchestra, thought that teaching elephants to play instruments would be difficult, but they picked it up in minutes.

the bigger picture!

Eye Can See You!

This alien-looking eye is actually the eye of a Panther chameleon! Every Panther chameleon has a different colorful pattern depending on where it comes from, and this guy lives in Madagascar. Wildlife photographer Daniel Heuclin, who has spent years traveling the world taking closeup photographs of animal eyes, captured this amazing eye in the wild.

Goats' eyes have rectangular pupils.

A giant squid's eye can be as large as a dinner plate!

Pampered Pets

Design for Dogs

Japanese designer Kenya Hara has commissioned well-known architects and designers to create homes and furniture for particular breeds of dogs for the Architecture for Dogs project. They include a mirror for a poodle, a hammock for a Jack Russell, a white, fluffy bed for a Bichon Frise, and ramps for a dachshund.

Lap of Luxury

Longcroft Luxury Cat Hotel in Hertfordshire, England, offers feline guests a luxurious stay while their owners are away. Cats enjoy designer beds and gourmet menus, including fresh cod, king prawns, and free-range chicken. Grooming services and entertainers complete the five-star service.

Refined Roost

Birdhouses seem to be getting fancier, and our feathered friends may soon be looking for realtors. This crazy cottage is one of a kind and has been compared to something from a Tim Burton movie. It was designed by Crooked Creations Birdhouses in Denver, Colorado.

Really?

A trailer has been made especially for dogs. It has wheels, a lockable door, interior carpeting, and matching wallpaper. Just ten have been made and they cost $5,000 each.

Style Statement

Some pet owners see their dog as a fashion accessory, but now dogs can have accessories of their own. Pawbags are exact miniature replicas of the designer bags carried by their owners, with price tags to match. An owner's bag and replica pawbag made by company VeryFirstTo costs from $500 to $5,000.

Cool, huh?

Tiny Tales

At two weeks, Beyoncé was just four inches long!

ACTUAL SIZE!

I'm a Survivor

When Beyoncé the puppy was born, she weighed just one ounce and could fit into a tablespoon. The dachshund crossbreed had no heartbeat and had to be resuscitated, so she was named after the pop star who sang "Survivor." Now the tiny dog lives at California's Grace Foundation as an "ambassadog," helping to promote the work of the animal welfare center.

Pint-Sized Pinto

A pinto stallion named Einstein weighed just six pounds and was only 14 inches tall when he was born at Tiz A Miniature Horse Farm in New Hampshire. Most tiny horses are dwarf breeds with short legs, but Einstein appears to be a normal, leggy foal.

Petite Piglets

Micro pigs weigh just nine ounces at birth and can sit inside a teacup, but these popular mini-pets come with a big price tag. A "teacup" pig costs $1,000 and does not stay teacup-size for long. The pigs eventually grow to the size of a large dog and can live for 20 years.

Chapter 3
Way to Live!

In High Places

Epic Escape

Anthony Martin parachuted safely into a field in Serena, Illinois, after being shackled inside a locked casket and tossed out of an airplane at 14,500 feet! His hands had been cuffed to a belt around his waist and his right arm was chained to the inside of the box. The Wisconsin daredevil has been specializing in amazing escapes since the age of ten.

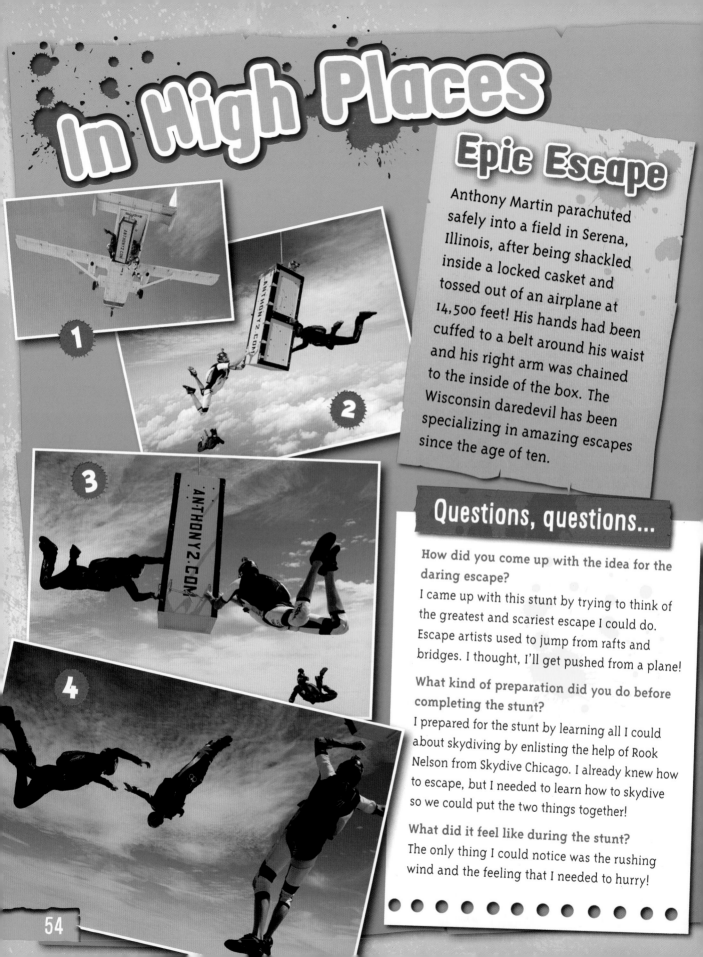

1

2

3

4

Questions, questions...

How did you come up with the idea for the daring escape?

I came up with this stunt by trying to think of the greatest and scariest escape I could do. Escape artists used to jump from rafts and bridges. I thought, I'll get pushed from a plane!

What kind of preparation did you do before completing the stunt?

I prepared for the stunt by learning all I could about skydiving by enlisting the help of Rook Nelson from Skydive Chicago. I already knew how to escape, but I needed to learn how to skydive so we could put the two things together!

What did it feel like during the stunt?

The only thing I could notice was the rushing wind and the feeling that I needed to hurry!

Money Raiser

Matt Silver-Vallance, who was born in South Africa, tied himself to 160 helium balloons and floated almost four miles across shark-infested waters off the coast of South Africa. He traveled from Robben Island, where Nelson Mandela was imprisoned, to Cape Town to raise money for the Nelson Mandela Children's Hospital.

Nerves of Steel

Extreme mountain biker Hans Rey took on the dangerous natural rock bridges of the Wadi Desert in Jordan, facing an unknown trail with a sheer drop at the end. The intrepid rider could have fallen at any moment from the eight story-high bridge, if he lost his line.

Really?

Musician Oz Bayldon, from London, England, raised almost $60,000 for a Nepalese orphanage by performing on top of a 21,830-foot mountain in the Himalayas.

Too Cool for School

Chilling Out

Surfers Dane Gudauskas, Alex Parker, and Keith Malloy swapped the warm waters of California for the Arctic surf of the Lofoten Islands, Norway, in search of monster waves. They wore two-inch-thick wet suits and had to wade through waist-high snow just to reach the sea.

One Cool Ride

This full-scale, working truck was sculpted from 14,000 pounds of ice on the frame of a Chevrolet Silverado, and then driven along the street at 12 miles per hour. The frozen pickup was featured in a commercial for a Canadian company to prove that its batteries were weatherproof at minus 40°F.

Snow Angels

Around 2,000 people laid down in the snow and flapped their arms and legs in unison as part of a charity event at the University of Minnesota, Duluth, that raised over $10,000 to provide clean drinking water for people in Ethiopia.

Really?

More than 30 truckloads of snow provided the ammunition for a mass snowball fight in Seattle, Washington. A total of 5,834 people took part to mark the city's Snow Day.

Slippery Stunt

Ryan Suchanek popped a wheelie traveling at more than 100 miles per hour on ice! And it's even more amazing since he lost his leg in a road accident in 2007, and became the only professional stunt rider with a prosthetic leg. Ryan rode on one wheel for more than 660 feet on frozen Lake Koshkonong in Wisconsin.

A Swedish man named Jonas got tattooed while free-falling at over 13,000 feet. It was the world's first free-fall tattoo.

the bigger picture!

Pyrotechnic Plunge

A team of Ohio-based skydivers have taken this extreme sport to a new level by attaching fireworks to their feet as they plummet to Earth from 13,500 feet. The fireworks burn at 3,000°F for about 45 seconds while the divers free-fall at speeds of up to 120 miles per hour. Then they release their parachutes—carefully avoiding the flames—before lighting another set of fireworks.

Really?

Miles Daisher has invented "skyaking"—skydiving while sitting in a kayak, then landing on water. Miles jumps from a plane in a short kayak, free-falls, then parachutes to land.

An Israeli hairdresser cut Sharon Har Noi's hair at 14,000 feet while the pair were skydiving.

Dan Knights did his first skydive with an instructor from 12,000 feet while solving a Rubik's Cube in less than 40 seconds.

Collection Crazy

Nest Collector

Wasps have fascinated Terry Prouty ever since he grew up in Louisiana, and he now owns a collection of more than 100 wasps' nests from around the world. Wasps build their impressive homes from chewed-up wood, and the average nest houses around 5,000 wasps.

Bzzzz...

The Real Thing

Coca-Cola can collector Davide Andreani, from Italy, has stacked up more than 10,000 cans, including one of the first produced in England in 1967, and designs from almost every country. The most valuable are those produced for a special event. The rarest gold cans can sell for up to $500.

Converse King

Joshua Mueller, from Lakewood, Washington, owns more than 1,500 different pairs of Converse shoes. They are not just for display, however—Joshua wears the sneakers, and has yet to wear the same pair twice.

Really?

Karen Bell, from Scotland, has been collecting Smurf figures and stickers for more than 30 years. She now has more than 5,000 items, which have cost her around $33,500.

Play House

Marlyn Pealane, from the Philippines, probably has more toys than your local toy store. Even though she lives in a small bungalow, Marlyn has a collection of more than 23,000 toys, and she sometimes invites the local kids to come and play with them for free.

Golf ball divers retrieve balls from golf course ponds, earning 5–10 cents per ball. They can collect 800,000 a year, but they work in dirty water and sometimes risk being bitten by snakes, alligators, or snapping turtles as they search through the mud.

Hair-Raising Offer

Hairstylists attracted a large crowd in the center of Changsha, China, when they offered free haircuts using a giant comb and a large pair of gardening shears. Few people wanted to take the risk, but one brave girl allowed them to cut her hair and said she was pleased with her new style.

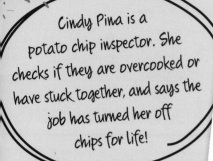

Cindy Pina is a potato chip inspector. She checks if they are overcooked or have stuck together, and says the job has turned her off chips for life!

Madeline Albrecht from Cincinnati, Ohio, had a job sniffing feet and armpits for 15 years, testing products to help smelly feet and pits!

Goose Guide

French ultralight pilot Christian Moullec rears barnacle geese at home and even lets them sleep in his bedroom. The endangered geese see Christian as their mother, so they follow him when he takes to the air. He is hoping to increase their numbers by guiding them to new habitats across Europe.

In the Balance

Head for Heights

Vadim Makhorov and Vitaliy Raskalov filmed themselves with head-mounted cameras as they scaled China's Shanghai Tower—the world's second-tallest building. It took the death-defying Russian climbers two hours to reach the one hundred and twentieth floor, and then they climbed the crane on top of the unfinished tower, reaching a height of 2,130 feet.

Skyscraper Scaler

A daredevil sky walker captured this stomach-churning selfie from the top of Dubai's Princess Tower—the world's tallest residential building. Alexander Remnev, age 19, from Moscow, Russia, scaled the 1,350-foot tower with friends during a vacation in this city of skyscrapers.

Balancing Act

A Chinese high-wire artist battled strong winds as he walked across a 50-foot slackline suspended between two hot-air balloons 100 feet above the ground. It took Saimaiti Aishan three-and-a-half minutes to complete the dramatic stunt, which took place in China's Hunan Province.

Really?

Hai-tank, a 91-year-old Shaolin monk from the Sil Lum temple in China, has been filmed performing amazing one-finger handstands!

Creak!

Rock Face Recliner

Dallin Smith from Provo, Utah, made a chair from leftover climbing rope and secured it 350 feet above the ground on a steep cliff at Rock Canyon. It took the skilled climber about four months to make the recliner, which he originally planned to put in his living room.

Amazing Kids

Inspirational Shepherd

Arthur Jones, from Dorset, England, cares for a flock of pedigree sheep and has won three prizes in county shows. Since he is the fifth generation in his family to be a shepherd, this is not surprising, but Arthur is just two-and-a-half years old and has cerebral palsy. Looking after the sheep has helped him to walk, and he herds them on a mini four-wheeler.

Superstrong Schoolgirl

Charley Craig was a slim 12-year-old girl, weighing just 84 pounds, when she managed to lift her own body weight above her head. Charley, from Glasgow, Scotland, started pumping iron at the age of nine. She comes from a family of weight lifters, and has already won both Scottish and British titles.

Really?

Tyler Armstrong, from California, was just nine years old when he reached the summit of Argentina's 22,837-foot-tall Mount Aconcagua.

Surfing Preschooler

At the age of three, Triston Gailey is already hanging ten. Triston, from California, first took to the water on a boogie board when he was just two years old. When his father noticed he was standing up on it, he bought him a surfboard, and they have been riding the waves ever since.

Footwear-Free

Hairstylist Richard Hudgins, from Kentucky, went barefoot for a year to raise money to buy shoes for children in Kenya. He started in December, so he had to endure freezing conditions before his feet became accustomed to the cold. He said his worst experience was walking on snow.

Belgian runner Stefaan Engels completed 365 marathons in as many days. He ran a total of 9,569 miles during the year, averaging four hours for each of his marathons.

Mark Beaumont cycled around the world in just 194 days and 17 hours. He completed the incredible 18,000-mile journey by cycling 100 miles a day.

Richard Roberts did something new every day for a year to raise money for charity, including drinking armadillo milk and rescuing a piglet.

Leighton and Charlotte Littlewood, Oli Vincent, and Carl Whittleston, from New Zealand, climbed all four of the highest peaks in the country's North Island in a single day to raise money for Parkinson's disease.

Wheee!

Topsy-Turvy Challenge

Julie Dumont, a Canadian student, decided to do a handstand every day for a year to raise money to build playgrounds in Uganda—all while completing a PhD at a college in Wales. She picked interesting locations for this daily task, including a plane's wing and on a sports track.

Helping Hands

Life-Saving Book

The Drinkable Book could save millions of lives. Its pages are water filters coated with minute particles of silver that kill bacteria, and each one can clean a 30-day supply of water. This means that a whole book can provide a single person with clean water for up to four years.

Beachcomber Beasts

Artist Gilles Cenazandotti, from the French island of Corsica, creates colorful life-size sculptures of endangered animals from plastic trash that he finds on the beach. His work highlights how animals struggle to survive in an environment threatened by trash and pollution.

Gilles has also created a polar bear and a dog from trash.

Cashing In

Irish artist Frank Buckley has built a house using blocks of old, shredded banknotes. Each block contains notes that were worth 50,000 euros, and the total value of the bills in the house was 1.4 billion euros ($1.82 billion). Even the pictures on the wall and the mattress were made with old notes.

Really?

Clean-energy campaigner Tom Weis pedaled a tricycle 2,500 miles across the United States, from Boulder, Colorado, to Washington, D.C., without consuming a drop of fossil fuel.

Group Hug

More than 2,000 people, including students, office workers, and Buddhist monks, hugged trees for two minutes in a park near Kathmandu, Nepal, while musicians beat traditional drums. They were celebrating World Environment Day by spreading awareness of the importance of trees.

Totally Extreeeme!

Living Dangerously

A group of daring kayakers braved water temperatures of 125°F as they came within feet of the red-hot lava flowing down from Kilauea volcano on the island of Hawaii. Brazilian daredevil Pedro Oliva tested the heat of the molten lava with his paddle, which immediately caught fire.

Really?

Gary Saavedra surfed a wave created by a boat traveling through the Panama Canal for almost four hours, covering a distance of 41.3 miles.

Jump Rope Masters

The longest jump rope marathon lasted 33 hours 20 minutes!

Li Jinlong, a pupil at Da Sun Ge Zhuang Central Elementary School in China, is shown here jumping an incredible 110 ropes. The students were practicing in preparation for a jump rope display to be performed at a sports cultural exhibition in the Chinese capital, Beijing.

Towering Achievement

Vittorio Brumotti climbed Dubai's Burj Khalifa, which at 2,716.5 feet is the world's tallest tower, by cycling up the stairs. The Italian cyclist rode up 3,700 steps and 160 floors, reaching the top in two hours and 20 minutes without once resting a foot on the ground.

Leap of Faith

Brave climber Kevin Jorgeson tackles giant boulders that are up to 16 feet tall without any ropes or harnesses, leaping from boulder to boulder between climbs. Kevin has climbed some of the toughest boulders in the world, some with ledges that are narrower and smaller than a credit card.

Hold on!

73

Chapter 4
Totally Bizarre

Home Comforts

Get Creative

The doodle duvet cover looks like a giant notepad and comes with a set of ten washable color pens, so it is perfect for jotting down late-night brain waves, creating an artistic masterpiece, or writing your own bedtime story. A quick wash will leave you with a blank sheet, so you can start over.

Really?

Furniture companies in Sykkylven, Norway, joined forces to build a sofa over half a mile long. It was displayed on a bridge spanning the wide Sykkylven fjord.

Gravity-Defying Home

A museum in Saint Petersburg, Russia, has turned the world on its head by creating an apartment where everything is upside down. Photos of visitors to the three-bedroom, two-bathroom home show them hanging from ceilings and performing fingerstands on the upside-down furniture.

A Taste for Fashion

This edible wardrobe and its contents were created by Steph Parker, from Birmingham, England, using vanilla, chocolate, and red velvet cake. The cake sculptor spent 40 hours making the wardrobe, which could feed more than 100 people. It even incorporates an iPad for online shopping!

Mural Masterpiece

Hardware store owner David Goldberg had a large collection of unwanted door parts, so he decided to upcycle it to re-create Vincent van Gogh's "Starry Night" on the wall of his store in Bethesda, Maryland. The mural is made up of 1,250 doorknobs and other pieces of hardware, and took four months to complete.

New York artist Henry Hargreaves creates mosaic portraits of celebrities using pieces of toast, some barely browned and others burned to a crisp.

Really?

Nathan Wyburn, a food artist from Wales, used crumbled crackers to re-create some of Britain's most famous faces, including the Duke and Duchess of Cambridge and One Direction's Harry Styles.

the bigger picture!

Citrus Celebration

The French town of Menton, on the Mediterranean coast, has been celebrating the end of winter with a lemon festival since the late nineteenth century. Each year, a different theme is chosen and the Biovès Gardens in the town center fills with giant figures made from 160 tons of oranges and lemons. The display shown here was based on Jules Verne's *20,000 Leagues Under the Sea*.

A promotion company created a giant iPhone 5 from fruit and vegetables (including apples).

Turkish artist Hasan Kale paints tiny cityscapes on foods, such as half an almond, pasta shells, and a coffee bean.

Love, Sweet Love

Rose Bowls

Chinese ceramic artist Wei Hua created a wall hung with hundreds of recycled toilet bowls, urinals, and sinks in Foshan, a city in Guangdong Province, China. He then filled them with 6,000 red roses in the shape of a heart to show his love for his new young bride.

Really?

Turkish couple Cengizhan Celik and Candan Canik exchanged their wedding vows via Twitter using an iPad.

Marriage Machine

The coin-operated AutoWed Machine offers couples the chance to tie the knot for less than the price of a pizza. Partners enter their names and take their vows using the keyboard, then the machine issues two plastic rings and a personalized wedding receipt—including a voucher for an auto-divorce.

How romantic!

Money Talks

Lok Tsao from Jiangsu Province, China, decided to propose to his girlfriend, but instead of saying it with flowers, he asked a florist to make a bouquet using 10,000 yuan ($1,600). It is against the law to cut or glue Chinese currency, so the florist folded the notes and clipped them in place.

Mateo Martinez proposed to his girlfriend at 20,000 feet—just before they skydived!

White Wedding

Susanne Grieve and Jeff Rawson met when they were working in Antarctica, braving temperatures of minus 76°F—so the *Antarctica: Empire of the Penguin* exhibit at SeaWorld in Florida was their perfect wedding venue. Guests included 250 penguins, perfectly dressed for the occasion in their black-and-white "tuxedos."

Brain Wave!

Crazy Dream

This skateboarding ramp floating on Lake Tahoe in the Sierra Nevada mountains was the wild idea of professional skateboarder Bob Burnquist. A diver was on hand to retrieve Bob's board as he put it to the test, and he finished the trial with a massive air jump off the ramp and into the lake.

PYO Berries

Instead of picking your own fruit, it may soon be possible to print it. A company in Cambridge, England, has developed a 3-D printer that drops tiny spheres of fruit gel in a pattern so that they form the shape of fruit like raspberries and blackberries.

Virtual Grocery Store

South Korean commuters who do not have time to shop can order their groceries while they wait for the train. A row of billboards at Seolleung subway station in Seoul displays photos of products with barcodes that shoppers scan using their smartphones. The goods are then delivered to their homes.

Grill and Chill

For a cookout with a difference, try the BBQ-donut. This circular boat seats ten and has a built-in charcoal grill in the center, which also converts to a cooler. A sunshade shields diners from the heat during the day, and colorful LED lights mean there's no need to head for shore when darkness falls.

Cornflake Creations

New York-based artist Sarah Rosado was inspired to create her first celebrity portrait from cereal when she was listening to music by John Lennon while eating breakfast. Since then, her subjects have included Alicia Keys, Madonna, Michael Jackson, and Rihanna (shown here). Each portrait takes about five hours to complete.

Anna-Sofiya Matveeva makes portraits from chewed gum. The Ukrainian artist needs up to 1,000 pieces per portrait, so she asks friends to chew the gum for her.

Jessica Dance's meals look good enough to eat, but they are all made from yarn. The British artist's knitted creations include hot dogs, a burger and fries, roast turkey, and a fried breakfast.

German artist Marco Figgen saves money by not buying paintbrushes and painting with the tip of his long beard instead.

Siberian Sand Sculptures

"My Favorite Film" was the theme for an exhibition of sand art, held in the Siberian city of Krasnoyarsk, Russia. Professional artists and students of Krasnoyarsk State Arts Institute created the exhibits, which featured characters from *Star Wars*, *Jurassic Park*, *Avatar*, and *King Kong*.

It Works?

Really?

English cyclists Pi Manson and James Lucas have built their own "double-decker" bikes, which stand six feet tall, by welding two frames together.

Chill-Out Music

A group of Swedish musicians named Ice Music perform on instruments hand-carved from ice by their founder, Tim Linhart. Performances take place in a giant "igloo," which is lit up to create a colorful display resembling the Northern Lights over Swedish Lapland.

Vegetable Orchestra

Brothers Nan Weidong and Nan Weiping grew up surrounded by vegetables on a farm in China's Anhui Province and their father was a music teacher, but it is only recently that they put the two together. Now they live in Beijing and create their own musical instruments using fresh vegetables.

Hilarious Helmets

A range of motorcycle helmets created by a team from Kazakhstan is guaranteed to turn heads as you ride your bike. The wacky designs include a cracked walnut, a globe, a watermelon, a tennis ball, a red onion, a brain, and a bald head with ears.

Massive Motorcycle

British plumber Colin Furze has built a 72-foot-long motorcycle that can seat 23 people, using one-and-a-half mopeds and an extended aluminum frame. He rode the bike without passengers for more than a mile at speeds of up to 35 miles per hour, but admitted that it is difficult to steer and turn.

Colin has also created superhero-like magnetic shoes so you can walk on the ceiling!

A bit bendy!

Yum, Yum

Munchable Masterpieces

Beau Coffron's kids must be the envy of the school cafeteria. The San Francisco father, aka Lunchbox Dad, puts other parents to shame with his movie- and holiday-themed packed lunches. They include a Snow Queen Elsa sandwich, a Kermit the Frog, and banana minions from *Despicable Me*.

The Art of Sushi

Japanese artist Tama-chan creates incredible art inside rolls of sushi—but until the roll is sliced, she never knows exactly how her artworks will look. She has produced more than 200 different sushi designs, using vegetables, seaweed, and colored rice.

Fun with Food

While most people choose the most perfect fruit and vegetables, Vanessa Dualib seeks out weirdly shaped produce that she can transform into cute creatures. The Brazilian artist has spent four years sculpting whales from eggplants and lobsters from sweet potatoes for her food art project *Playing with Food*.

A Bite to Eat?

Restaurant for the Brave

Watch out for sharp knives if you visit New York City's Ninja New York restaurant, located in an underground labyrinth representing a hidden ninja village. Servers attack diners with fake swords and entertain them with magic tricks, while dishes include soup cooked over 800°F rocks and seafood surrounded by smoking dry ice.

Eeek!

Camera Café

This giant vintage camera in a village in South Korea is actually a two-story café. The first floor includes a camera museum with exhibits ranging from antiques to tiny toys, and there is a photo gallery upstairs. Even the toilet paper is designed to look like a roll of film.

꿈꾸는사진기

Sci-Fi Servers

When diners arrive at this restaurant in Harbin, China, a robot greets them with the words "Earth person, hello. Welcome to the Robot Restaurant." Inside, robots wait tables, cook dumplings and noodles, and sing for the customers. Each robot costs $40,000 and works for five hours after a two-hour charge.

Dining on the Red Planet

At the Mars 2112 restaurant, on Broadway, in New York City, a UFO-like craft transported hungry humans to the Crystal Crater dining area, waiters were dressed in futuristic costumes, and a "teleporter" took diners back to the main floor after their meal. Sadly, the restaurant closed 100 years ahead of schedule in 2012.

Really?

There are no waiters at 's Baggers restaurant in Nuremberg, Germany. Customers order food using a touch screen and it arrives at the table via a roller coaster.

Looking Good

Finger Food

Food is always on hand with these incredibly detailed rings, created by British jeweler Rhonda Church. Rhonda started out making fridge magnets for friends, until news of her unique designs spread and she set up her online store. Each tiny meal can take up to 20 hours to make, and she can scent each piece to smell like the real thing!

Questions, questions...

How difficult is it to make your designs?

The pieces are difficult to make mainly because they are so small, so I have to wear special magnifying glasses. I also had to design and make my own tools to work the clay, as the tools I needed had not been invented. I have to use tiny tweezers just to lift some things into place.

How long does it take to make each piece?

Each piece takes between two to 20 hours to make, depending on the number of things that are on each plate. A donut is quicker to make than a plate of food, but because I try to make every item look real, I don't mind putting in the extra time to get it looking just right.

ACTUAL SIZE!

Boots with Bling

These boots are certainly not made for walking, since they are worth $3.2 million! Made in Belgium, they are decorated with 167 ounces of gold and 38,883 champagne, gray, and pink diamonds. It took 30,000 hours to make the boots and to select and set the diamonds.

Hair Hat

This horse-shaped hair hat, worn here at the Meydan racecourse in Dubai, is the work of Nagi Noda. The Japanese pop artist created a series of incredible animal-shaped hair sculptures, including a dog, an elephant, a bear, and a lion, using hair weaves, real hair, and wire.

Tuna eyeballs are regularly eaten in China and Japan. They are usually fried and served with rice and soy sauce.

Sannakji is a Korean dish of live octopus cut into pieces and eaten while the tentacles are still wriggling.

EATING HABITS

Bug Feast

British PhD student Peter Bickerton has a family history of heart disease, so he decided to reduce his own risk by replacing the meat in his diet with low-fat worms and insects. On a typical day, he eats locust oatmeal for breakfast, a cricket sandwich for lunch, and a tasty locust pizza for dinner as a treat.

Locust pizza!

Carnauba wax is usually found in the garage, where it is used to polish cars, but it is also an ingredient in gummy bears and fruit-flavored snacks.

The shiny coating on jelly beans is made from shellac, a resin made by the female lac bug, which is scraped from the bark of trees in India and Thailand.

Food Phobic

Hanna Little, from England, ate nothing but French fries for 15 years because she was terrified of all other foods. When she had to quit her job because she kept passing out, she was forced to take action. Now, after being hypnotized, she has eaten her first real meal—a pizza.

Chapter 5

Human Marvels

So Long!

Talon Queen

Despite having fingernails that are between 13 and 18 inches long, Lauren Curtis, from New Jersey, is an artist and jewelry maker, and regularly uses a computer keyboard. She has been growing her nails for more than 20 years, but keeps one thumbnail short for practical reasons. Lauren has appeared as "Talon the Nail Lady" at sideshows.

Questions, questions...

Have any of your nails ever broken off?
Yup! Most of them have broken at some time, but they usually break very high up on the nail so they're still long and I'm able to fix them with nail glue.

You are a full-time artist. How do you manage to create your art with your nails?
I'm just so used to having long nails that I'm able to draw, paint, do photography, and work on the computer without a problem.

Is there anything you cannot do because of your nails?
Really, the only things I can't do are things I never did or wanted to do, like bowling, darts, or skiing!

Every year Jiang's hair grows another eight inches!

Long Locks

In 1990, when Jiang Aixiu, from China's Henan Province, went to get her hair cut, the hairdresser suggested she should let it grow because it was in such good condition. Jiang followed that advice and her hair now measures almost 12 feet. It takes her two hours to wash.

Big Family

The four members of the Kulkarni family, from India, have a combined height of 26 feet. Former basketball player Sharad Kulkarni stands more than seven feet tall, while his wife and two daughters are all over six feet. They have had to modify their house and furniture, and order some of their clothes and shoes from Europe.

Height of an average adult man!

Ketchup Craving

British student Melissa Ibbitson has always loved ketchup. She goes through more than her body weight each year and eats it with almost every meal—even salad. Her birthday cake was shaped like a ketchup bottle and she gets ketchup-themed presents for Christmas.

King of Ink Land King Body Art The Extreme Ink-Ite (formerly Mathew Whelan) has covered 90 percent of his body in tattoos—he had his first ink at 16 and hasn't stopped since.

A Chinese girl named Bao Bao has been eating soil for 11 years. She developed this condition, known as pica, at the age of seven.

Kesha Davis, age 34, eats half a roll of toilet paper every day. She keeps a roll in her car and even sneaks sheets into the movie theater as a snack.

Watch it, I'm walking backward!

Peace Movement

In 1989, Mani Manithan decided to walk backward from his hometown in Tamil Nadu, India, to the city of Chennai, 300 miles away, to promote world peace. Since then, the cell phone shop owner has continued to walk backward and says that he has forgotten how to walk forward.

When she was a child, Lori Broady slept with a hair dryer running to drown out the noise of her large family. Now she has children of her own, but she still finds the humming of the dryer comforting and cannot sleep without it. Do not try this at home!

Superhumans

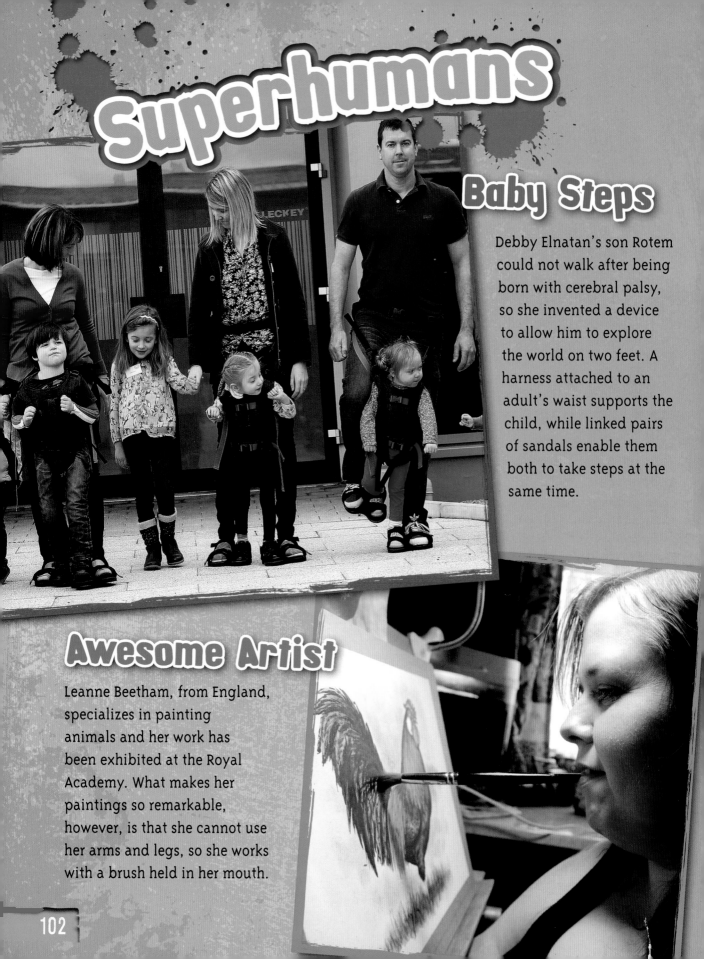

Baby Steps

Debby Elnatan's son Rotem could not walk after being born with cerebral palsy, so she invented a device to allow him to explore the world on two feet. A harness attached to an adult's waist supports the child, while linked pairs of sandals enable them both to take steps at the same time.

Awesome Artist

Leanne Beetham, from England, specializes in painting animals and her work has been exhibited at the Royal Academy. What makes her paintings so remarkable, however, is that she cannot use her arms and legs, so she works with a brush held in her mouth.

Real-Life Magneto

Etibar Elchiyev, nicknamed Magnetic Man, demonstrated his unusual ability by sticking 53 spoons to his chest and shoulders. The sports coach from Georgia, Eastern Europe, has even bigger ambitions and plans to move airplanes and train cars with his magnetic body in the future.

Really?

In 2011, 84 people in wheelchairs pulled a C-130 cargo aircraft weighing 74 tons almost 394 feet at a military airport in Belgium.

Bionic Arm

Former British soldier Andrew Garthwaite was fitted with a thought-controlled bionic arm after losing his right arm in Afghanistan. Surgeons took the nerve endings from his shoulder and rewired them into his chest muscles, so now his brain moves his prosthetic arm by focusing on the nerves in his chest.

How Do You Do That?

Whoosh!

Fling!

Super-Fit Senior

A German gymnast has proved that age is no barrier to keeping fit. Johanna Quaas gave up gymnastics when she had children and only started practicing again in her fifties. She was thinking of retiring until YouTube clips of her performing at the age of 86 became viral hits, with more than three million views. Since then, she has been stealing the show from her younger rivals with her impressive floor routines and displays on the parallel bars.

Heavy-Duty Hair

Circus performer Anastasia IV, who specializes in hanging by her hair, used her superstrong locks to pull a four-ton vehicle. She conditions her waist-length hair five times a day and two people spend 45 minutes braiding it like a rope before performances.

Really?

Lasha Pataraia from Georgia, Eastern Europe, pulled an 8-ton military helicopter for 70½ feet using a rope tied around his left ear.

Mighty Mouth

Dinesh Shivnath Upadhyaya has stuffed his mouth with everything from grapes to tennis balls over the years. The teacher, from Mumbai, India, recently fit five standard-size golf balls with a diameter of 1.68 inches each into his super-stretchy mouth and held them there for 55 seconds.

Gumph!

Art Forms

Finger Painting

British body painter Annie Ralli was commissioned to transform hands into buildings, sports scenes, brushes, and pens for an advertising campaign. She explains that she has to work quickly because paint is less stable on a living, moving base—and also because her "canvas" walks away at the end of the day.

Cutting-Edge Designs

Scalps are Paul Devlin's canvas of choice. The master barber from England specializes in creating razor-sharp patterns, including portraits and well-known cartoon characters, on the back of people's heads. Unfortunately, his clients can only admire his designs with the aid of a mirror.

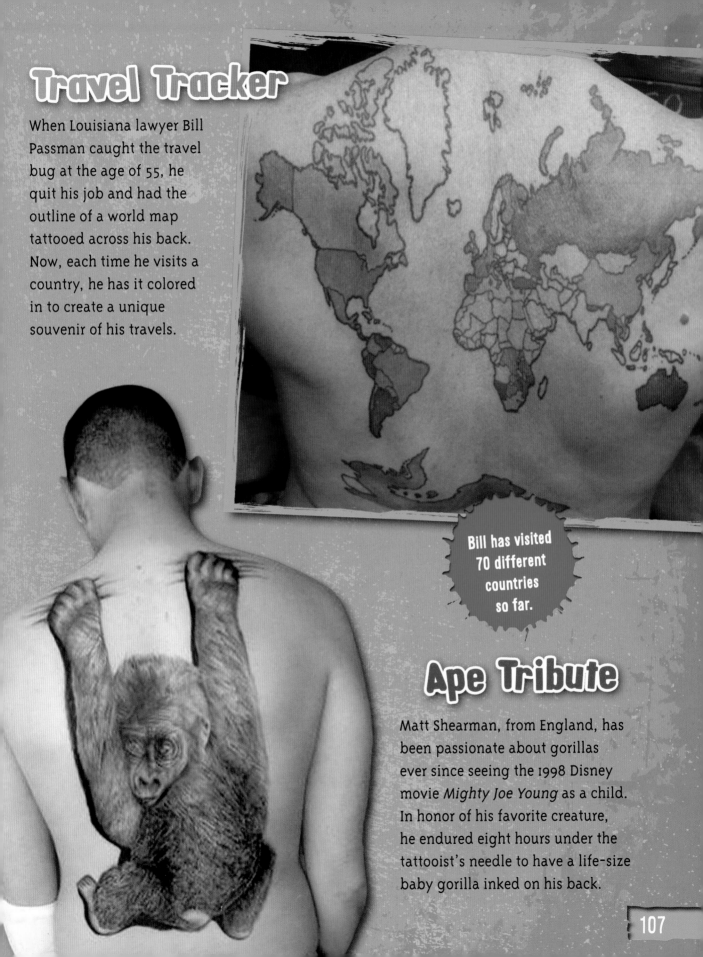

Travel Tracker

When Louisiana lawyer Bill Passman caught the travel bug at the age of 55, he quit his job and had the outline of a world map tattooed across his back. Now, each time he visits a country, he has it colored in to create a unique souvenir of his travels.

Bill has visited 70 different countries so far.

Ape Tribute

Matt Shearman, from England, has been passionate about gorillas ever since seeing the 1998 Disney movie *Mighty Joe Young* as a child. In honor of his favorite creature, he endured eight hours under the tattooist's needle to have a life-size baby gorilla inked on his back.

Every square inch of our skin is home to about 32 million bacteria. Luckily, most of them are harmless, and some are even useful.

Mighty Mustache

Mohammad Sadi's bright red mustache is a facial feature to be proud of for more than one reason. Mohammad, from Faisalabad, Pakistan, used it to pull a 1.9-ton truck a distance of 207 feet at a festival in the city of Lahore.

Odd Ears

Jack Window's ears appear to be upside down, as the fleshy part that should be at the bottom is at the top and other features are misplaced. Jack, from Worthing, England, says that his hearing is completely unaffected by his unusual ears.

We have five million scent receptors in our noses, while a dog has more than 220 million.

The Fugates, an isolated family that lived in the Kentucky hills in the early 1800s, had blue skin as a result of a rare condition called met-H. Their blood was not able to carry as much oxygen as normal, so it was darker and gave their skin a bluish tinge.

The human body contains about 60,000 miles of blood vessels. If they were laid end to end, they would stretch more than twice around the Earth.

Come Together

Two of a Kind

Around 375 pairs of twins, many identically dressed, gathered for a party organized by St. Thomas' Hospital, London, to celebrate the twenty-first anniversary of the Department of Twin Research. The twins have been taking part in medical studies to find out whether diseases and personality are a result of inherited genes or the environment we live in.

Seeing Red

Nearly 5,000 red-haired folk came together in the Dutch city of Breda to mark International Redhead Day. The two-day festival includes art, lectures, and workshops focused around red hair, and attracts redheads from over 80 different countries.

Mustache Meet

A total of 1,131 men with mustaches gathered on the ice following the Minnesota Wild ice hockey team's last home game in November 2010. It was part of the "Movember" charity event, which encourages men to grow mustaches during November to raise funds to fight men's cancers.

Really?

Irish twins Amy and Katie Elliott were born 87 days apart. Amy arrived four months early and miraculously survived, while Katie was born three months later.

Body P-arts

Hair-Raising

Before throwing away the hair from your brush, take a look at the work of Zaira Pulido. The Colombian artist takes long strands of human hair and uses them to embroider portraits and other images. Each portrait can take months, and takes lots of care and concentration. The results look like fragile pencil drawings.

Tooth Fairy Castle

Gina Czarnecki's "Palaces" sculpture is made of crystal-clear resin that will be encrusted with clusters of baby teeth. The British artist has invited children around the world to donate a baby tooth (while leaving a note for the tooth fairy) to help the sculpture grow into an incredible tooth fairy castle.

Pearly-White Gems

Australian silversmith Polly van der Glas creates jewelry using materials that were once part of the human body. Friends, strangers, and tooth fairies have donated the teeth she transforms into necklaces, rings, earrings, and cufflinks. She also makes pieces using hair and nails.

Really?

American artist Jenine Shereos creates fragile leaf sculptures using human hairs stitched together and secured with tiny knots.

Nail Feathers

American artist Laurel Roth Hope created these peacocks' fabulous feathers using hair clips and fake fingernails. There can be up to 3,000 nails in one sculpture and they have all been hand-filed and painted with three coats of polish. Each peacock takes between 300 and 400 hours to create.

Kim Do, a hairdresser from Vietnam, created a tunic with a matching hat made from 620 miles of human hair from 54 different people.

Really?

Australian graphic designer Josh Darrah shaved off his hair and glued it together to make a wig. He wore the wig to visit friends and family, then filmed their reactions as he pulled it off.

the bigger picture!

Inspired by Nature

Body painter Johannes Stoetter, who lives in Italy, transforms people into animals, fruits, and plants that are so realistic they are often mistaken for the real thing at first glance. His model here wore a swimming cap and put her head through a hole in a board after being painted as a pineapple. She was then photographed surrounded by real fruit.

Ariana Page Russell's sensitive skin allows her to create beautiful works of art on her own skin, by scratching or rubbing the surface in various shapes.

Holding a pencil in each hand, American artist Tony Orrico lies down on a canvas and spins his body around to create Spirograph-style drawings.

Family Portrait

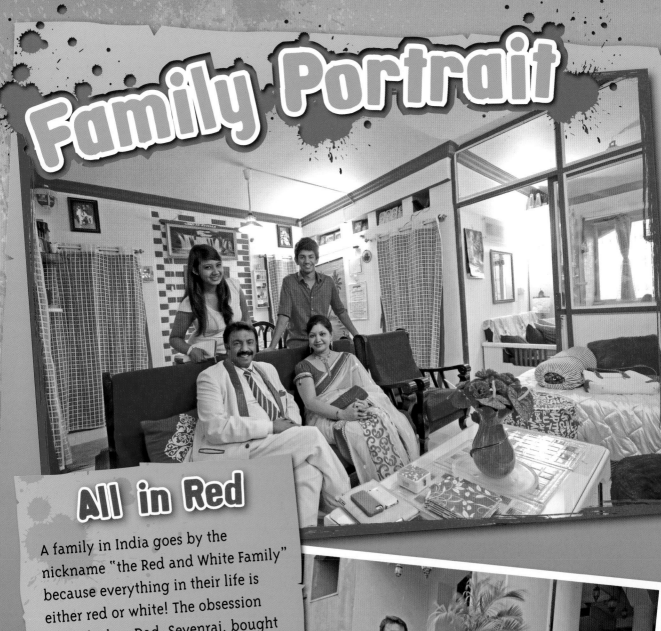

All in Red

A family in India goes by the nickname "the Red and White Family" because everything in their life is either red or white! The obsession started when Dad, Sevenraj, bought a red tie to go with his white clothes. He loved it so much he started decorating his house with the same color scheme. Even smaller items follow suit, including headphones, kitchen knives, and tablecloths. Sevenraj's wife, Pushpa, struggled with the colors at first, but his two children, Maneesha and Bharath, love the attention the family gets.

Family of Rapunzels

Tere Lynn Svetlecich Russell and her three daughters, from Illinois, have a combined hair length of more than 13 feet. Tere Lynn's hair measures 74 inches, and she has to wash it kneeling down because it drags her body to the floor when wet. Unsurprisingly, she and the girls are regular winners at State Fair ponytail contests.

Really?

British retiree Roy Blackmore was orphaned as a child, but after spending 28 years and about $33,500 tracing his roots back 1,500 years, he found almost 10,000 relatives.

3-D Mini-Me

British company iMakr is offering to create "mini-me" ceramic figurines using 3-D printing. Subjects step into a scanner, which produces a digital model that is then printed by applying ceramic powder in layers to build a solid object. The company claims the lifelike ornaments will add a new dimension to customers' mantelpieces and could be popular as personalized wedding cake toppers.

Chapter 6
Over the Top!

Sunday Best

Sole Food

Twin brothers Remigijus and Egidijus Praspaliauskas from Lithuania have designed a collection of edible, wearable shoes made of bread. Every pair is unique and colors range from white to brown bread. The loafers are perfect for keeping toes toasty, but the designers warn that they are not suitable for wet weather.

Really?

A chocolate handbag is one of the exhibits on display at China's World Chocolate Wonderland theme park in Shanghai.

Sawdust Dress

Sofia de la Rocha was asked to make a garment out of recycled materials that were not like fabric as part of her course at the Rhode Island School of Design. She created this dress, inspired by rocks eroded by rushing water, using sawdust mixed with glue and resin.

Creature Features

Unleash the animal within with one of these eye-catching T-shirts. The creatures' unbelievably lifelike, 3-D faces certainly jump out at you. The designs include animals ranging from a cute Chihuahua or a cuddly kitten to a hissing red mamba snake or snarling sabertooth tiger.

Ew, hope it doesn't rain!

Matching Coats

Some say that dog owners often look like their pets and that is certainly true of people who knit sweaters using their dogs' fur. Doumé Jalat-Dehen, from France, spins yarn from her clients' dog hair, but owners need to start collecting early because it takes about seven years to gather enough for a sweater.

Crazy Contests

Frogfest

The Croatian village of Lokve is surrounded by marshes, which are home to many frogs. Each spring, the residents hold a celebration called Frog Night, which includes a frog-jumping contest. Competitors are not allowed to touch their frogs, so they encourage them to leap the farthest by blowing on them or making loud noises.

Nettle Nosher

Ouch!

British chef Phillip Thorne ate the leaves from 40 long stalks of stinging nettles to win the World Nettle Eating Championship, which took place in Dorset, England. Competitors strip and eat the leaves from two-foot-long stalks, which are then counted to find the winner.

Bridal Rivals

Married and single women from Estonia put on wedding gowns and make a dash for the finish line in the annual Runaway Brides competition. The winner receives a golden ring and the title of the "Most Runaway Bride." In 2014, a total of 73 women raced on a 55-yard grass track on the grounds of a thirteenth-century fort in the town of Narva.

Really?

Japanese air guitarist Nanami "Seven Seas" Nagura won the 19th Air Guitar World Championships in Oulu, Finland, after impressing the judges with her energetic performance.

Underwater Artistry

Most jack-o'-lantern carvers do not have to worry about their pumpkins floating away, but that can be a problem when Halloween preparations take place 25 feet below the surface of the ocean. This underwater pumpkin-carving contest took place in the Florida Keys National Marine Sanctuary off Key Largo.

Dozens of volunteers helped make a giant taco stretching 134 feet as part of a festival to promote the Plaza Garibaldi district of Mexico City.

15 INCHES TALL!

the bigger picture!

Meat Fest

Standing 15 inches tall and 24 inches wide, this monster snack would challenge even the most committed carnivore. The sandwich weighed over 28 pounds and contained 40 layers of meat including beef, duck, chicken, turkey, ham, venison, salami, bacon, sausage, and chorizo. It was created by British chef Tristan Welch to mark the launch of the TV show *Man v. Food Nation*.

Joey Chestnut managed to eat 141 hard-boiled eggs in eight minutes in October 2013!

Visitors to the Kansas Relays in Lawrence, Kansas, feasted on a 4,689-pound nacho platter that was 2 feet wide, 10 inches deep, and 80 feet long—the same length as two school buses!

Fan-Atics!

Magical Memorabilia

Katie Aiani from California has spent more than $65,000 collecting Harry Potter memorabilia over the past 16 years, and even has part of a handwritten letter she received from J.K. Rowling tattooed on her arm. She is so fanatical about the films and books that she has traveled to set locations, Quidditch matches, and film premieres.

Katie's special tattoo.

Kitty Kingdom

Natasha Goldsworth has collected more than 10,000 pieces of Hello Kitty merchandise, including jewelry, clothing, furniture, kitchenware, and 4,000 stuffed toys. The 29-year-old's tiny apartment in Devon, England, is filled to the brim with the items, which have cost her more than $80,000.

DIY Batmobile

Batman megafan Zac Mihajlovic spent two years building a Batmobile in his backyard in Sydney, Australia. He bought about a third of the parts from the actual car used by the Caped Crusader in the 1989 movie and molded the rest at home. He now uses the car for professional and charitable purposes—and occasionally to pick up the groceries.

Remarkable Revamps

Trash to Cash

Arizona artist Jeff Ivanhoe recycles discarded aluminum cans by cutting them into tiny pieces and arranging them to create mosaic images that range from vintage cars to a portrait of the Statue of Liberty. The AluMosaics take two to three weeks to complete and sell for thousands of dollars.

Recycled Cycles

There are estimated to be 300 million bicycles in China, so a huge number are scrapped each year. This unique 39-foot-tall Christmas tree on display at a shopping mall in Shenyang, Liaoning Province, shows an imaginative way of reusing them. It is made of more than 230 bicycles.

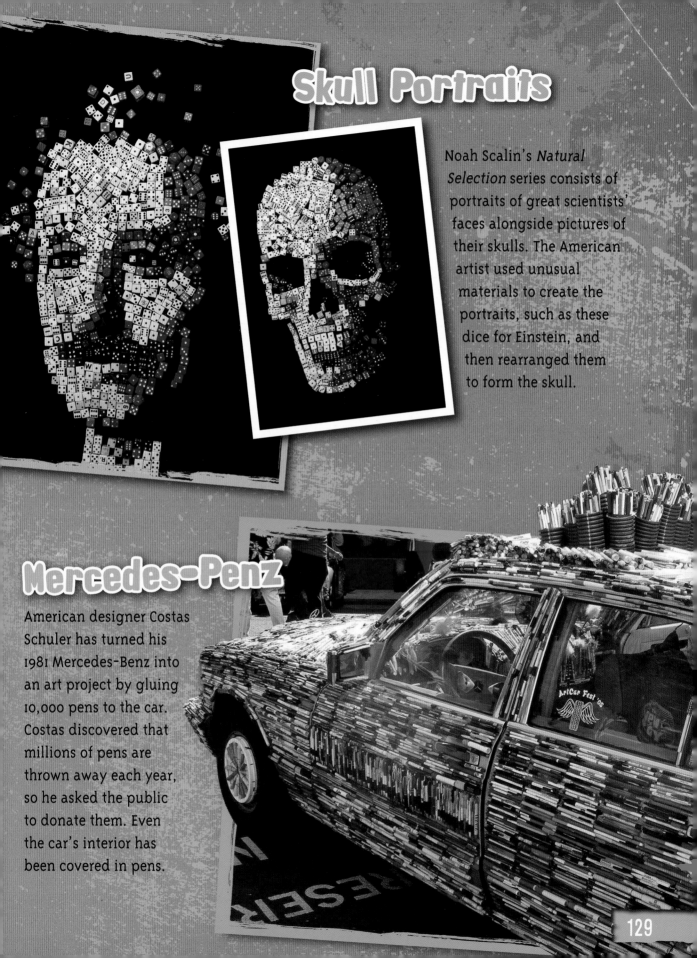

Skull Portraits

Noah Scalin's *Natural Selection* series consists of portraits of great scientists' faces alongside pictures of their skulls. The American artist used unusual materials to create the portraits, such as these dice for Einstein, and then rearranged them to form the skull.

Mercedes-Penz

American designer Costas Schuler has turned his 1981 Mercedes-Benz into an art project by gluing 10,000 pens to the car. Costas discovered that millions of pens are thrown away each year, so he asked the public to donate them. Even the car's interior has been covered in pens.

129

Artist Ben Wilson paints miniature masterpieces on pieces of chewing gum that litter the sidewalks of London, England.

Every summer in Águeda, Portugal, the Umbrella Sky Project hangs hundreds of colorful umbrellas with string above the streets, bringing a shower of color and providing shade.

Paper Pandas

French artist Paulo Grangeon displayed 1,600 papier-mâché pandas outside Taipei City Hall in Taiwan in February 2014. The exhibition, called Pandas on Tour, first launched by the World Wildlife Fund in 2008, reminds people that there are only about 1,600 giant pandas living in the wild.

Potato Protest

German artist Peter Pink placed a group of potatoes wearing sunglasses and waving banners outside a railway station in Berlin, Germany. He wanted to create a potato protest and this is just one of his pieces featuring vegetables in sunglasses. He's also made an army of cucumbers and a French fry funeral.

Twenty-four colorful giant snails made from recycled plastic were installed in Sydney, Australia, to highlight the need for recycling to protect the environment.

Artist Mademoiselle Maurice used 30,000 paper origami sculptures to decorate streets in Angers, France.

Pick a Team!

Hole New Game

FootGolf is one of the fastest-growing sports in the world. It combines the popular games of soccer and golf and is as simple as it sounds. Players kick off from a tee box and try to get their soccer balls into a 21-inch-diameter hole using the fewest number of kicks.

Really?

Golfers can play all night with light-up golf balls. The LED light is activated when the ball is hit and shines for eight minutes after each shot.

Swoosh!

Waterskiing with a Twist

Chuck Patterson is equally at home on a surfboard or on skis, so it's not surprising that he decided to give wave-skiing a try. The extreme athlete from California was towed to the peak of a wave by a Jet Ski, then rode down it on his custom-made skis.

Playing Dirty

Swamp soccer is said to have originated in Finland, where it was used as a training exercise for athletes and soldiers. There are six players on the boggy field and the game is played in two halves, each lasting just 13 minutes because it is so physically demanding.

Horsing Around

The sport of horseboarding was invented by British brothers Daniel Fowler-Prime and Tom Kilroy when they were messing around with friends and tied a rope between a horse and a mountain board (like a skateboard, but the wheels have tires). Boarders are pulled along at up to 40 miles per hour and the sport relies on teamwork between the horse, the rider, and the boarder.

Good Enough to Eat

Rainbow Uni-Cake

Food curator Miss Cakehead and the Tattooed Bakers got together to celebrate National Baking Week in 2013 by creating a completely edible landscape, including a life-size unicorn cake! The tasteful creature was filled with rainbow-colored cake layers and adorned with edible gold leaf-embossed hooves and a horn.

Sweet Star

This portrait of Marilyn Monroe, made from 2,100 bite-size, stuffed cupcakes, was displayed next to her wax figure in New York in 2012. The eight-foot-by-four-foot picture of the actress, who died in 1962, was unveiled on the eve of what would have been her eighty-sixth birthday.

Coffee Gets Personal

Some coffee chains label coffee cups with customers' names, but Let's Café in Taiwan has taken personalized coffee to a new level. The coffee chain offers customers the option of uploading a selfie from their smartphones and seeing it re-created in edible powder on top of their coffee foam.

Cubist Art

Artist Brendan Jamison from Northern Ireland uses sugar cubes as building blocks and bonds them together with special glue. His sweet structures have included London's Tate Modern gallery, which used 71,908 cubes, and Bangor Castle Town Hall in Northern Ireland, shown here, which features a clock tower and detailed windows.

Are You Kidding?

Dream Dad

When your dad works as a special-effects artist for DreamWorks, anything is possible. Animator Daniel Hashimoto has used his CGI skills to turn his son James into an action movie hero. The videos of the toddler's adventures, called Action Movie Kid, see James using a grappling gun to shoot up to the ceiling, destroying a toy display with a lightsaber, crossing a lake full of lava, and blasting off into space.

Questions, questions...

We talked to Daniel about what it's like to create Action Movie Kid...

How did you come up with the idea?
I have always loved creating visual effects as a hobby since I was in grade school. Now that I'm a dad, I'm constantly shooting home videos of my son. One day, I thought it'd be really fun to add some effects to show my son—who loves superheroes. I posted them online, and the whole thing went viral.

How does James react when he sees the final videos?
James loves them. He laughs, yells, and jumps around with excitement after each new video. James now knows that the videos are pretend, but it doesn't stop him from playing big, and even requesting me to make videos out of his playtimes.

Ultimate Playhouse

The Master Wishmakers make children's dreams come true. The British company builds luxury playhouses, and if a house is not enough, there are shops, garages, beach houses, gas stations, and princess castles, too, with prices ranging from $45,000 to $90,000. They have even built an entire pirate's island.

Really?

A treetop palace could be yours for just $400,000. British company Blue Forest builds luxury tree houses featuring obstacle courses, hot tubs, and security.

Made of clay!

Global Cuisine

English designers Joe Shervell and Chris Morley spent two days re-creating 40 national dishes from around the world using modeling clay. They included an American hamburger, Swedish meatballs, Peking duck from China, French crêpes, and English fish and chips.

Wheely Good

Crazy Cars

Sudhakar Yadav, from Hyderabad, India, has become world famous for his wacky, road-legal vehicles made from scrap. His designs include cars in the form of a bed, a billiard table, a camera, lipstick, and a high-heeled shoe, as well as an eggplant-shaped camper van.

In the Fast Lane

Three British car enthusiasts bought an old coin-operated van, from the popular British children's TV series *Postman Pat*, and fitted it with wheels and a 500cc motorcycle engine. Now, the former children's ride reaches speeds of more than 100 miles per hour and puts supercars such as the Porsche 968 to shame.

Cramped Camper

This tiny RV has just four foot by four foot of living space, but still manages to squeeze in four seats, a stove, a sink, a table, and a bed. English custom car fanatic Andy Saunders built the tiny camper by combining a pedal cart with an old two-berth mobile home.

Comin' through!

Really?

When Dutch artist Wouter van den Bosch was given a tractor tire, he built a 1,650-pound bicycle around it. He often rides the huge, heavyweight bike around his hometown of Arnhem.

Wheeled Luggage

After forgetting his luggage one day, He Liangcai, from China's Hunan Province, came up with the idea of creating a suitcase that doubles as a scooter. The electric vehicle carries two people and reaches speeds of 12 miles per hour. It has GPS, a theft alarm... and plenty of storage space.

Index

Photo Credits

Ripley Entertainment Inc. and the editors of this book wish to thank the following photographers, agents, and other individuals for permission to use and reprint the following photographs in this book. Any photographs included in this book that are not acknowledged below are property of the Ripley Archives. Great effort has been made to obtain permission from the owners of all material included in this book. Any errors that may have been made are unintentional and will gladly be corrected in future printings if notice is sent to Ripley Entertainment Inc., 7576 Kingspointe Parkway, Suite 188, Orlando, Florida 32819, USA.

COVER PHOTOS ©: Squid, Richard E. Young/Tree of Life web project/tolweb.org; bubbles, tunart/iStockphoto; background, Photocreo Bednarek/Fotolia.

BACK COVER PHOTOS: © t, Robert Eikelpoth/Galeries/Corbis; br, Fancy/Media Bakery; bl, mjooo7/Getty Images; background, Photocreo Bednarek/Fotolia

CONTENTS PAGE: 2: Anthony Martin skydive escape—Anthony Martin Skydive Chicago Book "Escape or Die"; Golf balls in mouth—Dinesh Shivnath Upadhyaya; **3:** Wedding vending machine—Sam Lanyon; Toys in Space—Nicolas Lamorelle; Food rings—Rhonda Barrow-Church from NeatEats Jewelry

INTRO PAGE: 6: Jimi Hendrix portrait—Used with permission of Ed Chapman; **7:** Ice wheelies—Mike Nightengale - Photographer; Winter the dolphin—Clearwater Marine Aquarium; Long nails—Image owned by Lauren Curtis

CHAPTER 1: 10: Foam surfing—Rex/Chris Garden/Solent News; Giant hailstones—Caters News Agency; **11:** Lumps of ice—Alexey Trofimov/Solent News/Rex; Lightning strikes the Grand Canyon—Rolf Maeder/Rex; **12:** Bioluminescent sea—Doug Perrine/SeaPics.com; Ice cave—All rights reserved Sergey A. Krasnoshchekov 2007-2011; **13:** Firefly swarm—Steve Irvine/ Solent News; Lava watching—Denis Budkov/SellYourPhoto. net; **14:** Custard Pie Championship—PA Wire/Press Association Images; **15:** Mud Festival—Kim Jae-Hwan/Staff; The Zombie Walk—Demotix/Press Association Images; **16:** Gingerbread house—Supplied by Wenn.com; **17:** Plane house—From AirplaneHome.com, republished with permission; **18:** Igloo hotel—www.iglu-dorf.com; Napping pods—Zuma/Rex; **19:** Underwater hotel room—Genberg Art UW Ltd/Jesper Anhed/ Rex Features; Sandcastle hotel—LateRooms.com and Mischief PR; **20-21:** International Ice and Snow Sculpture Festival— Getty Images; **22:** Cliff journey to school—HAP/Quirky China News/Rex; Sequoia National Park—Amy Selleck; **23:** Toys in Space—Nicolas Lamorelle; **24:** Dragon hedge— Geoff Robinson Photography/Rex; Giant tree roots—Photo by Coke Smith; **25:** Giant tree sculpture—Kim Beaton at PalTiya. com; **26:** Mystery Falls—Stephen Alvarez/National Geographic; **27:** Lost city underwater—Europics/CEN; The flooded valley— © Keren Su/China Span/Alamy; **28:** Dolphin island—Photo Fabrice Fourmanoir; Polar bear-shaped rock—2002 © Sanjay Jhawar; **29:** Dragon iceberg—Kseniia Maiukova/Sellyourphoto. net; Snow-covered trees—Sergey Makurin/Sellyourphoto.net

CHAPTER 2: 32: Big fish—Neil Cook/BNPS; Giant rat— HAP/Quirky China News/Rex; **33:** Giant jellyfish—Bob Cranston/ SeaPics/Solent; Dog with long tongue—Josh Edelson/AFP/ Getty Images; **34:** Snake in hood of car—Caters News Agency; Bird with fish in mouth—Christopher Schlaf/Solent News/ Rex; **35:** Chicken in tree—Quirky China News/Rex; Dog and elephant—www.MyrtleBeachSafari.com; **36:** Winter the dolphin—Clearwater Marine Aquarium; **37:** Owl on kayak— Pentti Taskinen/Rex; Goat with wheels—edgarsmission.org.au; **38:** Desk safari—desksafari.tumblr.com; **39:** Cat Afro (top two images)—Louise Cannatella, Michelle Foster michelle_ cbtinternet.com; Cat Afro (bottom image)—April Ann Coble; **40:** Boy with marmot friend—Caters News Agency; **41:** Bear in the house—Heidi and Hans-Juergen Koch/eyevine; Pet rhino—Alexey Tishchenko/SellYourPhoto.net; **42:** Glow-in-the-dark fish—© Pichi Chuang/Reuters; Squid with teeth—Richard E. Young/Tree of Life web project/tolweb.org;

43: Panda cow—AP/Press Association Images; Scary spider— Caters News Agency; **44:** Skateboarding cat—Supplied by Wenn.com; Dog in plane—Matt Power/Rex; **45:** Surfing pig—Caters News Agency; Elephant orchestra—Getty Images; **46-47:** Close-up Panther chameleon eye—NHPA/Photoshot; **48:** Architecture for dogs—Photographer Hiroshi Yoda/Rex; Hotel for cats—Barcroft Media via Getty Images; **49:** Luxury birdhouse—www.paigeeden.com; Pawbags—VeryFirstTo.com/ Rex; **50:** Tiny dog on iPhone—Getty Images/Moment RF; Tiny dog on hand—© Max Whittaker/Reuters; **51:** Tiny horse—AP/ Press Association Images; Micro pigs—Geoff Robinson

CHAPTER 3: 54: Anthony Martin skydive escape—Anthony Martin Skydive Chicago Book "Escape or Die"; **55:** Cliff riding— Dean "Blotto" Gray/GT Bicycles; Balloon journey—© Stringer/ Reuters; **56:** Arctic surfer—Caters News Agency; Ice truck— Canadian Tire/Rex; **57:** Snow angels—AP/Press Association Images; Ice wheelies—Mike Nightengale - photographer; **58-59:** Fireworks skydive—Caters News Agency; **60:** Wasp nest collector—Wenn; Coca-Cola can collector—Davide Andreani; **61:** Converse collector—www.flickr.com/photos/ thatconverseguy; Toy collector—Toys; **62:** Hairdresser with large comb—Quirky China News/Rex; **63:** Bird pilot—Jeremy Durkin/Rex; **64:** Climbing China's second tallest building— Caters News Agency; Dubai selfies—Caters News Agency; **65:** Hot-air balloon slackline—Quirky China News/Rex; Seat on cliff face—Photo: Dallin Smith Subject: Matt Spencer; **66:** Young shepherd—Bournemouth News/Rex; **67:** Young weight lifter—Laurentiu Garofeanu/Barcroft Media; Young surfer—Joe Johnston/AP/Press Association Images; **68:** No shoes for a year—AP/Press Association Images; **69:** Handstand a day for a year—Julie Dumont/Rex; **70:** Life-saving book—Photo by Solent News/Rex; Beach litter sculpture—Gilles Cenazandotti/ Rex Features; **71:** House made of money—© Cathal McNaughton/ Reuters; Tree-hugging—© Navesh Chitrakar/Reuters; **72:** Lava kayaking—Alexandre Socci/Barcroft Media; Skipping rope jumping—© Zhang Naijie/Xinhua/eyevine; **73:** Cycling up Burj Khalifa—Andrea Oddone—Brumotti.com; Boulder climbing— Caters News Agency

CHAPTER 4: 76: Doodle duvet cover—DoodleByStitch/Solent News/Rex; Upside-down house—© Alexander Demianchuk/ Reuters; **77:** Cake wardrobe—Caters News Agency; Door furniture art—David Goldberg; **78-79:** Octopus made of oranges and lemons—© Olivier Anrigo/Reuters; **80:** Toilet bowls with heart-shaped roses—Stringer/Imaginechina; Wedding vending machine— Concept Shed Ltd. www.conceptshed. com; **81:** Proposal with banknotes—EuroPics[CEN]; Married with penguins—Supplied by Wenn.com; **82:** Floating skate ramp—Visit California/Solent News/Rex; Print your own fruit—Dovetailed/Rex; **83:** Virtual shopping—Paul Brown/ Rex; Inflatable BBQ boat—Solent News/Rex; **84:** Cornflake art—Sarah Rosado; **85:** Sand art—© Ilya Naymushin/Reuters; **86:** Ice instruments—Graeme Richard/Wenn.com; Vegetable instrument—Reuters; **87:** Bald head helmet—good.kz/Rex Features; Long motorcycle—Geoffrey Robinson/Rex; **88:** Lunchbox designs—Beau Coffron www.lunchboxdad.com; **89:** Sushi art—Title: "Smiling Sushi Roll" © Tama-chan Online store: http://www.littlemore.co.jp/enstore/products/detail; Food world—Vanessa Ackel Dualib; **90:** Ninja restaurant—Caters News Agency; Camera café—Caters News Agency; **91:** Robot restaurant—Reuters; Mars restaurant—Wenn.com; **92:** Food rings—Rhonda Barrow-Church, owner and creator of NeatEats Jewelry; **93:** Expensive boots—© Benoit Tessier/Reuters; Horse hair wig—© Jumana El-Heloueh/Reuters; **94:** Locust pizza— Mathew Growcoot/News Dog Media; **95:** Living on fries— Caters News Agency

CHAPTER 5: 98: Long nails—Image owned by Lauren Curtis; **99:** Long hair—Quirky China News/Rex; Tall family—Shariq Allaqaband/Cover Asia News; **100:** Addicted to ketchup—Caters News Agency; **101:** Walking backward—Caters News Agency; **102:** Harnesses for children—William Cherry/Rex; Amazing artist—Caters News Agency **103:** Magnetic man—© David Mdzinarishvili/Reuters; Prosthetic arm—PA Archive/Press Association Images; **104:** Grandma gymnast—Steve Meddle/ Rex; **105:** Pulling car with hair—PA Archive/Press Association Images; Golf balls in mouth—Dinesh Shivnath Upadhyaya; **106:** Finger art—Getty Images; Hair art—Caters News Agency; **107:** World map tattoo—Caters News Agency; Gorilla tattoo— swns.com; **108:** Pulling truck with beard—AFP/Getty Images; **109:** Upside-down ear—Jack Window; **110:** Twins lineup— OnEdition Media; Twins gathering—Getty Images; **111:** Redhead gathering—EPA/Bas Czerwinski; Mustache gathering—Bruce Kluckhohn, Minnesota Wild; **112:** Human hair art—Zaira Pulido/ Colombian Artist; Tooth fairy castle—Dave Thompson/PA Wire; **113:** Teeth earrings—Artwork by Polly van der Glas, www. vanderglas.com.au Photographs: James Morgan & Terence Bogue; Fake fingernail peacock—Laurel Roth Hope and Gallery Wendi Norris Photo by Andy Hope; **114-115:** Body art—WB Production Johannes Stoetter; **116:** Red and white family— Jagadeesh K.R/Cover Asia Press; **117:** Long hair family—Travis Haughton/Barcroft Media; 3-D portraits—3-D Printed Mini-You's from iMakr.com

CHAPTER 6: 120: Bread shoes—Rex; Sawdust dress—Sofia de la Rocha http://portfolios.risd.edu/sofiadelarocha; **121:** Pet T-shirts—Used with permission of themountin.com; Dog fur clothes—Untitled-from the Dogwool serie © Erwan Fichou, 2007; **122:** Frog-jumping contest—AFP/Getty Images; Nettle eating contest—Caters News Agency; **123:** Runaway Brides competition—Caters News Agency; Underwater pumpkin carving—© HO/Reuters/Corbis; **124-125:** Giant meat sandwich— Rex; **126:** Harry Potter fan—Katie Aiani; **126-127:** Batmobile—Zac Mihajlovic; **127:** Hello Kitty fan—swns.com; **128:** Can art—Jeff Ivanhoe; Christmas tree made of bicycles—Photoshot; **129:** Skull portraits—Noah Scalin/Rex; Car covered in pencils—Costas Schuler/Solent News/Rex; **130:** Paper pandas—Reuters/Patrick Lin; **131:** Potato protest—Peter Pink/Rex; **132:** FootGolf—Reuters; Skiing on waves—Greg Huglin/Solent News/Rex; **133:** Swamp football—Quirky China News/Rex; Horseboarding—Jeremy Durkin/Rex; **134:** Unicorn cake—Tattooed Bakers www. tattooedbakers.com, image by Baker and Maker; Marilyn Monroe made of cupcakes—Erik Pendzich/Rex; **135:** Coffee portraits— Reuters; Sugar cube building—Courtesy of Brendan Jamison www.brendanjamison.com; **136:** Action Movie Kid—Daniel Hashimoto "Action Movie Kid"; **137:** Ultimate playhouses—The Master Wishmakers; Clay food—Caters News Agency; **138:** Shoe car—AFP/Getty Images; Fast Postman Pat van—Stu Stretton's photos; **139:** Cramper van—BNPS.co.uk; Suitcase bike—Reuters